9/02

D1188270

Stone Cold
Pro Wrestler
Steve Austin

by Michael Burgan

Reading Consultant:
Dr. Robert Miller
Professor of Special Education
Minnesota State University, Mankato

CAPSTONE
HIGH-INTEREST
BOOKS

an imprint of Capstone Press
Mankato, Minnesota

Capstone High-Interest Books are published by Capstone Press
151 Good Counsel Drive, P.O. Box 669, Mankato, Minnesota 56002
http://www.capstone-press.com

Library of Congress Cataloging-in-Publication Data
Burgan, Michael.
 Stone Cold: pro wrestler Steve Austin/by Michael Burgan.
 p. cm.—(Pro wrestlers)
 Includes bibliographical references and index.
 ISBN 0-7368-0920-1
 1. Austin, Steve, 1964—Juvenile literature. 2. Wrestlers—United
States—Biography—Juvenile literature. [1. Austin, Steve, 1964- 2. Wrestlers.]
I. Title. II. Series
GV1196.A97 B87 2002
796.812'092—dc21
[B]   00-013075

Summary: Traces the personal life and career of professional wrestler "Stone Cold"
Steve Austin.

Editorial Credits
Angela Kaelberer, editor; Lois Wallentine, product planning editor;
 Timothy Halldin, cover designer and illustrator; Katy Kudela, photo researcher

Photo Credits
Albert L. Ortega, 10, 24, 40
AP/Wide World Photos, 35
Dr. Michael Lano, 13, 15, 16, 18, 21, 22, 29, 30
Duomo/CORBIS, 4
PRNewsFoto, 36
Reuters/JIM BOURG/Archive Photos, 7
Rich Freeda/WWF Entertainment via Liaison Agency, cover, 26
Russell Turiak/Liaison Agency, 42
Steven E. Sutton/Duomo/CORBIS, cover inset photos, 32, 39

Capstone Press thanks Dr. Michael Lano, WReaLano@aol.com, for his assistance
in the preparation of this book.

1 2 3 4 5 6 07 06 05 04 03 02

Table of Contents

Chapter 1

WWF Champion

It was March 29, 1998. Nearly 20,000 pro wrestling fans filled the Fleet Center in Boston, Massachusetts, for WrestleMania 14. Many more fans watched on TV.

In the last match, "Stone Cold" Steve Austin would wrestle Shawn Michaels for the World Wrestling Federation (WWF) World Championship. Michaels was the current WWF World Champion.

Wrestlers play a role during their matches. Some are heroes. They also are called "babyfaces" or "faces." Other wrestlers act mean to their opponents and the fans. They are known as "heels." Michaels was the heel at

Steve wrestled Shawn Michaels at WrestleMania 14.

WrestleMania 14. Steve was the face. Most of
the fans cheered for him.

A Special Match

Michaels led a group of heels known as
D-Generation X. Members of the group were
at the match to help Michaels. These wrestlers
included Paul Levesque and Joanie Laurer.
Levesque is known as Hunter Hearst Helmsley or
Triple H. Laurer wrestles as Chyna. Boxer Mike
Tyson also was there to support Michaels. Steve
had no one to help him.

Michaels started the match by hitting Steve.
Steve fought back. He threw Michaels over the
ropes. Michaels landed on top of Triple H. Steve
followed Michaels out of the ring. Triple H then
started fighting Steve. The referee forced Triple H
and Chyna to leave the area near the ring.

The action continued both inside and outside
of the ring. Tyson picked up Steve and threw him
back into the ring. Michaels then tried to put a
sleeper hold on Steve. During this move, a
wrestler tries to cut off the flow of blood to
the opponent's head. This action can cause the
opponent to pass out briefly.

Boxer Mike Tyson helped Steve win his match against Shawn Michaels at WrestleMania 14.

Steve was able to escape the sleeper hold by backing Michaels into the ropes. During this move, Michaels hit the referee and knocked him out. The match went on without a referee.

Michaels prepared to use his signature move. This move is called Sweet Chin Music. During this move, Michaels kicks his opponent's chin. But Steve caught Michaels' foot before it hit his chin.

Steve then used his own signature move. It is called the Stone Cold Stunner. Steve stood in front and slightly to the side of Michaels. He wrapped his arm around Michaels' head. He then dropped to his knees as he slammed Michaels to the mat.

Steve covered Michaels to pin him. But there was no referee to make the three-count. Tyson then entered the ring to act as the referee. Tyson was no longer helping Michaels. Instead, Tyson made the count as Steve pinned Michaels. Steve was the new WWF World Champion.

About Steve Austin

Steve Austin is 6 feet 2 inches (188 centimeters) tall and weighs 252 pounds (114 kilograms). His real name is Steve Williams. Steve sometimes is called "the Texas Rattlesnake." He was born in Texas and still lives there.

Steve started wrestling in 1989. He won his first wrestling championship in 1991. Steve has won the WWF World Championship five times and the WWF Intercontinental Championship twice. Steve also has won the WWF Tag Team Championship four times.

Major Matches

March 2, 1993—Steve wins the WCW Tag Team Championship with partner Brian Pillman.

December 27, 1993—Steve defeats Dustin Rhodes to win the WCW U.S. Championship.

June 23, 1996—Steve wins the WWF King of the Ring competition.

August 3, 1997—Steve defeats Owen Hart to win the WWF Intercontinental Championship.

March 29, 1998—Steve defeats Shawn Michaels for the WWF World Championship.

June 29, 1998—Steve defeats Kane to win his second WWF World Championship.

March 28, 1999—Steve defeats The Rock to win his third WWF World Championship.

June 28, 1999—Steve defeats the Undertaker to win his fourth WWF World Championship.

April 1, 2001—Steve defeats The Rock to win the WWF World Championship for the fifth time.

Chapter 2

The Early Years

Steve Austin was born December 18, 1964, in Victoria, Texas. His name was Steve Anderson when he was born.

Steve's parents divorced when Steve was very young. Steve's mother's name is Beverly. Beverly later married a man named Ken Williams. Steve chose to use his stepfather's last name.

Steve grew up in Edna. This small town in southern Texas has about 5,500 people. As a boy, Steve liked to watch pro wrestling matches on TV. He cheered for his favorite wrestlers. His parents did not share his interest

Steve was born and grew up in Texas.

in wrestling. They told him to turn off the TV and go outside to play.

High School and College
In high school, Steve was popular with his classmates. He liked to have fun and tell jokes during classes. But he also was a good student. Steve was named to the National Honor Society. This group's members include the top students at high schools throughout the United States.

Steve played two sports at Edna High School. He threw the discus for the track team. On the football team, Steve played fullback on offense and linebacker on defense.

Steve graduated from high school in 1983. He then attended Wharton County Junior College in Wharton, Texas. The college offered him a scholarship to play football. The scholarship paid for Steve's college expenses. He played at Wharton for two years.

Steve then won another scholarship to play football for North Texas State University in Denton. This college now is called the University of North Texas. Steve studied

Kerry Von Erich

As he grew up, Steve often watched Fritz Von Erich and his sons wrestle.

Fritz Von Erich's real name was Jack Adkisson. He was from Dallas. Von Erich began wrestling in the 1950s. His championships included three National Wrestling Association (NWA) U.S. Heavyweight Championships and two NWA World Heavyweight Championships. His signature move was called the Iron Claw.

Von Erich later started World Class Championship Wrestling (WCCW). Steve briefly wrestled in the WCCW in 1989. Von Erich's sons also wrestled for the WCCW in the 1970s and 1980s. The sons were David, Mike, Chris, Kevin, and Kerry. Like their father, they won several wrestling championships.

physical education. He also played defensive lineman on the football team. He tackled runners and tried to stop quarterbacks from throwing the ball.

Steve injured his knee during his last year at North Texas State. He still managed to play well. But Steve knew that he was not good enough to play professional football. He also wanted to take some time off from school. He left school in 1987 without earning a degree.

A Career in Wrestling

Steve found a job working at a warehouse. He loaded and unloaded trucks. His bosses liked the way Steve worked. They wanted to give him a better job and put him in charge of other workers. But Steve did not want this job. He had been thinking about a new career. Steve thought that he could be a successful wrestler.

In 1989, Steve saw an ad for a wrestling school. A wrestler named "Gentleman" Chris Adams ran the school. Steve signed up for the school. He already was strong and in good

Steve met Jeannie Clark in Texas. They later married.

shape. But he needed to learn wrestling skills. Steve worked with Adams for a few months.

Becoming Steve Austin

World Class Championship Wrestling (WCCW) hired Steve after his graduation from wrestling school. This wrestling company was based in Dallas, Texas. Late in 1989, Steve wrestled his first match. He beat Frogman LaBlanc in Dallas. Shortly after, Steve began

Steve joined the WCW in 1991.

wrestling for the United States Wrestling Alliance (USWA). He wrestled in Texas before moving to Tennessee.

Steve was still using his real name in the ring. In Tennessee, he learned that there was another wrestler named Steve Williams. The man who organized the wrestling match told Steve to make up a new last name. Steve could not think of anything that he liked. The promoter called him "Steve Austin."

Steve did not wrestle well during his first match in Tennessee. The promoter told him to study other wrestlers. Steve noticed how they put different moves together. He saw how they tried to get the fans interested in the match.

Steve had a hard life as a wrestler. He made only $20 for each match. But his wrestling skills improved. Wrestling promoters began to notice him. In 1990, *Pro Wrestling Illustrated* (PWI) magazine named Steve the Rookie of the Year. Steve received this award for being the best new wrestler in 1990.

Marriage and the WCW

In 1989, Steve met Jeannie Clark in Texas. Jeannie sometimes worked as Steve's valet. Valets are women who walk to the ring with wrestlers. They also cheer for and help the wrestlers during matches. Jeannie and Steve later married.

In 1991, World Championship Wrestling (WCW) contacted Steve. At the time, this large wrestling company was based in Atlanta, Georgia. WCW officials wanted Steve to work for the company. Steve was moving up in the world of professional wrestling.

Chapter 3

First Championships

Steve began wrestling in the WCW as "Stunning" Steve Austin. Most wrestlers wear a costume in order to interest the fans. Steve did not wear a costume. He wore wrestling shorts and black boots. But Steve looked different than he does today. He had long, blond hair.

Early Championships

On June 3, 1991, Steve beat Bobby Eaton for the WCW Television Championship. This title was a minor one in the WCW. But Steve held

Steve was known as "Stunning" Steve Austin during his early days in the WCW.

the title for nearly one year. On April 27, 1992, Steve lost the title to Barry Windham. On May 5, he defeated Windham to regain the title. But he lost it in September to Richard Blood. This wrestler is known as Ricky Steamboat.

Steve later won a more important title in the WCW. In December 1993, he defeated Dustin Rhodes for the U.S. Championship. Steve held that title for eight months. In August 1994, he lost the title to Steamboat. Steve won and lost the title again in September.

These titles were important to Steve's career in the WCW. But Steve's greatest WCW fame came as a member of a tag team called the Hollywood Blonds.

The Hollywood Blonds

Steve's partner in the Hollywood Blonds was Brian Pillman. Like Steve, Pillman had long, blond hair. Pillman was 6 feet (183 centimeters) tall and weighed 226 pounds (103 kilograms). He was small compared to many other wrestlers. But he was quick. Pillman was known as "Flyin' Brian" because of his

Brian Pillman was Steve's partner in the Hollywood Blonds tag team.

speed in the ring. Steve and Pillman teamed up after Steve lost the Television Championship for the second time. They quickly became one of the WCW's best tag teams.

The Hollywood Blonds wrestled for the WCW Tag Team Championship on March 2, 1993. They faced Steamboat and Troy Martin. Martin was known as Shane Douglas. At one point, Pillman was losing to Steamboat.

Steve wrestled in Japan in 1994.

Outside the ring, Steve grabbed the Tag Team Championship belt. He hit Steamboat with the belt. Steve then helped Pillman pin his opponent. The Hollywood Blonds were the new Tag Team Champions.

Steve had cheated to win that night. He and Pillman sometimes cheated in other matches. They also sometimes argued with each other. The Hollywood Blonds were heels. But they were popular with fans.

The Hollywood Blonds lost their title on August 18, 1993. Pillman was hurt and could not wrestle that night. Darren Matthews took his place. Matthews wrestled as Lord Steven Regal. Steve and Regal lost the title to Marty Lunde and Paul Centopani. These wrestlers are known as Arn Anderson and Paul Roma.

Soon after, the WCW decided to break up the Hollywood Blonds. Steve was angry about this decision. But he accepted it. Steve and Pillman sometimes wrestled against each other. They remained good friends outside of the ring.

Leaving the WCW

In 1994, Steve went to Japan to wrestle. There, he had an accident in the ring. Steve jumped off the ropes in the corner of the ring. His opponent moved the wrong way. Steve landed hard on the mat. He tore a muscle in his right arm.

Steve continued to wrestle in Japan. But his arm still hurt. Doctors fixed the muscle when Steve returned to the United States. Steve then had to rest so that his arm could heal. During this time, the WCW decided that they did not want to pay Steve. They fired him.

Steve shaved off his hair after he joined the WWF.

In September 1995, Steve joined Extreme Championship Wrestling (ECW). This wrestling company was based in Philadelphia, Pennsylvania. But Steve could not wrestle right away. His arm was still healing. Steve appeared at matches and talked about wrestling. He sometimes made fun of other wrestlers or the WCW. Steve later wrestled a few times in the ECW as "Superstar" Steve Austin.

The WWF

Vince McMahon is the owner of the WWF. In late 1995, McMahon offered Steve a job with the WWF. McMahon and his assistants gave Steve a new name. They called him "The Ringmaster." Steve also looked different. He cut his hair very short. He later shaved off all his hair.

Steve did not like wrestling as The Ringmaster. He worked with a manager named Ted DiBiase. At matches, Steve did not get to talk as much as he had in the ECW. DiBiase often spoke for him. Steve asked McMahon if he could create a new character for himself.

Steve had watched a TV show about murderers. He saw how cruel these killers were. They did not care about anyone. Steve was not a cruel person. But he liked the idea of playing someone who did not care about other people. Steve's new character would do whatever he wanted to do.

Steve needed a name for his new character. One day, his wife made him some tea. She told Steve to drink it before it turned "stone cold." Jeannie's remark gave Steve an idea. He decided that his new character's name would be "Stone Cold" Steve Austin.

Chapter 4

The WWF

Steve had his next major match on June 23, 1996. He wrestled at a WWF event called King of the Ring. He first faced "Wildman" Marc Mero. Steve accidentally bit himself in the lip during the match. He later needed 18 stitches to close the cut. But Steve defeated Mero.

In the final match, Steve faced Aurlian Smith Jr. Smith wrestles as Jake "The Snake" Roberts. The winner of the match would be the King of the Ring. Roberts had injured his ribs earlier in the night. Steve was able to pin him in less than five minutes.

Roberts talked about religion after his matches. He often referred to the Bible verse John 3:16.

Steve quickly became one of the WWF's most popular wrestlers.

After this match, Steve made up his own saying. He made fun of Roberts for losing the match. Steve told Roberts that he had "whupped" him. Steve called his saying "Austin 3:16."

A New Star

The King of the Ring title made Steve famous in the WWF. He began to develop his "Stone Cold" Steve Austin character. He acted as if he hated everyone in the arena. Steve also came up with the Stone Cold Stunner.

Steve was acting as a heel. He thought that fans would not like him. But the fans cheered for Steve. Many wore T-shirts with "Austin 3:16" on them. These shirts became the most popular shirts sold by the WWF.

Steve won his first WWF Championship on May 26, 1997. He wrestled in a tag team with Shawn Michaels. They defeated Owen Hart and David Smith for the Tag Team Championship. Smith was known as Davey Boy Smith or the British Bulldog.

Steve and Michaels did not remain partners for long. In July, Steve teamed with Mick Foley. Foley was then known as Dude Love. Foley also

Steve's Austin 3:16 shirts became the most popular shirts sold by the WWF.

sometimes used the names Cactus Jack and
Mankind when he wrestled. Steve and Foley
won the Tag Team title from Hart and Smith.

On August 3, 1997, Steve faced Owen Hart
for the WWF Intercontinental Championship.
Hart tried a move called a piledriver. He
picked up Steve and held him upside down.
Steve's head was between Hart's knees. Hart
then dropped Steve headfirst onto the mat.

Rivals in the Ring: The Hart Foundation

Steve had some of his best matches against the Hart Foundation. Bret "The Hitman" Hart led this group of wrestlers. It included Brian Pillman, Davey Boy Smith, Jim Neidhart, and Hart's younger brother, Owen Hart.

Bret Hart

Bret Hart came from a family of Canadian wrestlers. He wrestled for the WWF from 1985 to 1997. During that time, he won the WWF World Championship five times. He also won two WWF Intercontinental Championships and three WWF Tag Team titles. Bret later wrestled for the WCW. He won two WCW World Championships.

Owen Hart also was a well-known wrestler. He won three WWF Tag Team Championships. On May 23, 1999, Owen died from an accident in the ring. He was 33 years old.

I was lying there helpless. I was paralyzed
for a minute...it was a scary thing.
—Steve Austin, *Ottawa Sun*, 11/10/97

Wrestlers know how to do this move so that
the other wrestler does not get seriously hurt.
But Hart made a mistake that night.

Steve hit the mat hard. He lay still on the
mat for almost one minute. He slowly moved
his fingers. He then moved his legs. Steve
went on to win the match. But he had seriously
injured his neck. Doctors told him that he
might have to quit wrestling.

Steve took time off from wrestling. He lost
his Tag Team and Intercontinental titles. But he
remained popular with the fans. In November
1997, Steve returned to wrestling. He won
back the Intercontinental belt by beating Hart.
Steve was now ready to wrestle for the WWF
World Championship.

WWF Champion

In March 1998, Steve defeated Michaels
to win the WWF World Championship. Steve
also gained a new rival. Vince McMahon
sometimes wrestled or worked as a referee.

Steve and McMahon sometimes became angry with each other during matches. The fans loved to see Steve arguing with his boss.

Steve held the World Championship belt for three months. He lost it on June 28 to Glen Jacobs. Jacobs wrestles as Kane. The next night, Steve won back the title from Kane.

In September, Steve defended his title during a three-way match. His opponents were Kane and Mark Calloway. Calloway is known as the Undertaker. Kane and the Undertaker pinned Steve. He lost the title. But *Professional Wrestling Illustrated* still named him the Wrestler of the Year. Steve won this honor again the next year.

Title Changes

In 1998, wrestler Rocky Maivia was winning most of his matches. Maivia is known as The Rock. On March 28, 1999, The Rock was the WWF World Champion. Steve faced The Rock at WrestleMania 15.

Steve wrestled The Rock at WrestleMania 15.

The Rock and Steve wrestled for nearly 30 minutes. The two men dragged each other outside of the ring and back again. They knocked out three referees as they wrestled. The Rock took Steve down with the Rock Bottom. The Rock stood next to Steve. He wrapped his arm around Steve's head and neck as he pulled him into the air. The Rock then slammed Steve's head and upper body down to the mat. Steve was able to get up. He used the Stone Cold Stunner on The Rock. Steve then pinned him to win the title.

In May, Steve lost the World Championship to the Undertaker. Steve won the title back from the Undertaker in June. In August, Steve wrestled in another triple threat match. His opponents were Mankind and Triple H. Mankind won the match and the title.

Steve wore padding on his knees for that match. But during the match, Triple H hit him on the knees with a chair. Steve decided he needed another break from wrestling. He continued to appear on TV and tried to wrestle

In August 1999, Steve wrestled in a Triple Threat match at SummerSlam.

a few times. But he usually was in a great deal of pain.

In November 1999, Steve learned that he needed an operation to fix his neck injury. Steve spent most of 2000 recovering from this operation. But he still appeared at WWF matches. During one match, he helped The Rock win the WWF World Championship.

Chapter 5

Steve Austin Today

The WWF used Steve's surgery as part of its TV shows. The storyline said that another wrestler had run Steve down with a car. For months, Steve and the WWF tried to find the car's driver. The story was not true. But it kept fans interested in Steve as he recovered from his surgery.

In September 2000, the WWF said that wrestler Rikishi had run down Steve. Rikishi's real name is Solofa Fatu. Rikishi and Steve then faced each other in Albany, New York, on October 22, 2000. The match was declared a no contest. Neither wrestler won. Steve's fans were just glad to see him back in the ring.

Steve appeared on the TV show *Nash Bridges* while he recovered from surgery.

> I've got some more to give to wrestling.
> I'll know when it's time to walk away.
> Right now isn't the time.
> —Steve Austin, *Dallas Morning News*, 9/23/00

The Royal Rumble

On January 21, 2001, Steve wrestled in his first major event since he returned to wrestling. He competed in the Royal Rumble in New Orleans, Louisiana. This event involved 30 wrestlers. One wrestler would enter the ring every two minutes. The last wrestler standing would win the event.

Steve was the 27th wrestler to enter the ring. Only Steve, The Rock, and Kane were left in the ring near the end of the match. Steve threw The Rock out of the ring. Kane and Steve continued to wrestle until Steve took Kane down with a Stone Cold Stunner. Steve then hit Kane three times with a chair and threw him out of the ring. Steve was the winner of the Royal Rumble.

A Champion Again

On April 1, 2001, Steve had a chance to win the WWF World Championship. He wrestled The Rock for the title at WrestleMania 17.

Steve has won five WWF World Championships.

This event took place at the Astrodome in Houston, Texas.

Steve and The Rock wrestled for nearly 30 minutes. They traded punches both inside and outside of the ring. Later in the match, Steve used the Rock Bottom twice on The Rock. He followed these moves with a Stone Cold Stunner. Steve then hit The Rock with a chair for the pin. Steve had won his fifth WWF World title.

Steve married Debra McMichaels in September 2000.

Life in Texas

Steve lives on a ranch near San Antonio, Texas. He enjoys driving his pickup truck and listening to music. Steve likes heavy metal and country music. Steve also hunts deer.

Steve spends time at his ranch with his two daughters. Stephanie was born in 1992. Cassie

was born in 1996. Their mother is Jeannie
Clark. Jeannie and Steve divorced in May
1999. Steve and Jeannie both help raise
their daughters.

In September 2000, Steve married again.
His new wife is Debra McMichaels. In the
past, Debra worked as a valet and wrestled in
the WWF. She held the WWF Women's
Championship for about one month in 1999.
Debra still works for the WWF. She often
appears on the company's TV shows.

Outside the Ring
Steve does other work besides wrestling. He
helps the WWF design T-shirts and other items
with his name on them. Fans buy "Stone Cold"
hats, jackets, and toys. Steve earns money from
these items.

Steve also acts. He appeared on the TV show
Nash Bridges. Steve played a police officer
named Jake Cage. Steve may do more acting in
the future. But he plans to spend most of his
time wrestling. Steve wants to be remembered
as one of the greatest wrestlers of all time.

Career Highlights

1964 — Steve is born December 18 in Texas.

1983–1986 — Steve plays football for Wharton County Junior College and North Texas State University.

1989 — Steve wrestles for World Class Championship Wrestling (WCCW) and the United States Wrestling Alliance (USWA).

1991 — Steve joins the WCW.

1995 — Steve joins the WWF.

1996 — Steve wins the WWF's King of the Ring competition.

1998 — Steve wins his first two WWF World Championships.

1999 — Steve wins two more WWF World Championships.

2000 — Neck surgery keeps Steve from wrestling until late in the year.

2001 — Steve wins the Royal Rumble competition and his fifth WWF World Championship.

Words to Know

opponent (uh-POH-nuhnt)—a person who competes against another person

promoter (pruh-MOH-tur)—a person who organizes events such as concerts and wrestling matches

referee (ref-uh-REE)—a person who makes sure athletes follow the rules of a sport

rookie (RUK-ee)—a first-year athlete

scholarship (SKOL-ur-ship)—a grant of money that helps a student pay for education costs

signature move (SIG-nuh-chur MOOV)—the move for which a wrestler is best known; this move also is called a finishing move.

valet (VAL-ay)—a person who walks to the ring with a wrestler and helps the wrestler during matches

To Learn More

Alexander, Kyle. *Pro Wrestling's Most Punishing Finishing Moves.* Pro Wrestling Legends. Philadelphia: Chelsea House, 2001.

Burgan, Michael. *The Rock: Pro Wrestler Rocky Maivia.* Pro Wrestlers. Mankato, Minn.: Capstone High-Interest Books, 2002.

Ross, Dan. *Steve Austin: The Story of the Wrestler They Call "Stone Cold."* Pro Wrestling Legends. Philadelphia: Chelsea House, 2000.

Sherman, Josepha. *Stone Cold Steve Austin.* Sports Files. Chicago: Heinemann Library, 2001.

Useful Addresses

Extreme Canadian Championship Wrestling
211 20701 Langley Bypass
Langley, BC V3A 5E8
Canada

World of Wrestling Magazine
Box 500
Missouri City, TX 77459-9904

World Wrestling Federation
  Entertainment, Inc.
1241 East Main Street
Stamford, CT 06902

Internet Sites

Canadian Pro Wrestling Hall of Fame
http://www.canoe.ca/SlamWrestling/
   hallofame.html

Professional Wrestling Online Museum
http://www.wrestlingmuseum.com/home.html

Stone Cold.com—Steve Austin
http://www.stonecold.com

WWF.com
http://www.wwf.com

Index